CHASING THE FRUIT TREE

A Book of Prayer and Affirmation

VICKIE V KNOX

Copyright © 2022 by Vickie V Knox
All rights reserved.
ISBN: 978-0-578-89417-1

Introduction

When we come to God with humility only seeking to express gratitude, and thankfulness just as we are, because there will never be perfection in man. Romans 3:23 ESV for all have sinned and fallen short of the glory of God. Roman3:10 ESV. None is righteous, no not one.

Dedication

To my Son Kevin seek God first and everything else will
come with a promise.

To my Granddaughter Tyeashia.
God is the ultimate promise keeper and the greatest friend and confidant.
Stay close to the Lord at all times.

Instilled in me by my parents Clifford and Helen Turner,
You taught me to carry Corinthians 13:13 as my being.

For my brother Clifford Jr. Micah 7:18-19

FIRST FRUIT GOD REMEMBER

O' God, thanks for the coming of spring for the world, and the constant of the Shekinah Glory for us! Shekinah's Glory is the manifestation of God on earth, whose presence is seen through natural things.

Shekinah is Hebrew, meaning "dwelling or one who dwells speaking to God's divine presence. God, thanks for the description of the word Shekinah because it's not in the Bible.

Shekinah means to reside or stay forever, the presence of God amongst his people:
Exodus 19:16-18,
Exodus 40:34-38
1st kings 6:13- as a cloud
Exodus 24:16-18
Exodus 33:9
1st kings 8:10-3 - as a pillar of smoke and fire
Exodus 13:21-22, as fire and a burning bush
Zechariah 2:5
Exodus 3:2
Thank You, God, for mentioning Shekinah Glory in Exodus after the Israelites left the shackles of slavery in Egypt; Exodus 13:20-22.

Thank you, God, for your declaration of your glory among the people 1st Chronicles 16:24 and 2nd Corinthians 4:6.

O', God, thank You for being You; God and man in one person, just for our sins.

Hebrews 2:17, Thank You, God, for the ultimate due season that's constant with no changes. Glory to God.

It is in Jesus name I pray, Amen.

FIRST FRUIT GOD REMEMBER

God, we ask right now that you bind the spirit of restlessness, the stronghold the devil has devised to keep us from sleeping period. O', God, please help us rest, casting all anxiety on you.

1st Peter 5:7 God, you've told us in your word you will keep us in perfect peace, if we trust you." "Trust in the Lord forever, for the Lord himself is an eternal rock. Isaiah 26:3-4.

So Father God, we thank You for sweet sleep,

Proverbs 3:24. Father no tossing and turning from when we can't sleep; no medicine- just powerful prayer; a renewing of our bodies, mind, spirits.

God, please send the archangel Gabriel into our dreams with messages of healing, and to help us become healthier as a whole.

God, help us remember to pray about whatever is worrying us when we can't sleep.

O' God, give us the faith we need to trust that You will intervene in any situation we give to You in prayer.

Thank You for always being here with us and loving us unconditionally and completely, knowing that we can rest because of our relationship with you.

It is in Jesus name I pray, Amen.

FIRST FRUIT GOD REMEMBER

IS IT EASTER OR RESURRECTION SUNDAY?

Saints of God, there is a term in the urban dictionary that explains being woke. Woke means being aware, knowing what's going on in the community, related to racism and social injustice. The word *"woke"* has a long history of words and phrases that relate; the gaining of knowledge, to sleep or to see or being blind to the truth or is needed to open our eyes.

Lord, thank You for our woke experience. In John 11:25- 26, Jesus said," I am the resurrection and the truth, and the life, the one who believes in me will live, even though they die; and whoever lives by believing in me will never die. Do you believe this?

Thank You Lord for our woke experience (repeated)
Acts 4: 33; with great power, the apostles continued to testify to the resurrection of the Lord Jesus and God's grace was so powerfully at work in them all.

Thank You God for the or our woke experience of 1st Peter 1: 3: "Praise be to God and Father of our Lord Jesus Christ! In great mercy, He has given us new birth into a living hope through the resurrection of Jesus Christ from the dead.

Happy *"Woke"* Resurrection Sunday.
It is in Jesus name I pray, Amen.

FIRST FRUIT GOD REMEMBER

Saints of God, since its Easter in the world, I am reminded of the story about the Hare and the Tortoise. Slow and steady wins the race.

Lesson 1: Learn from failure- a test for the testimony
1st John 4:4 you, dear children, are from God and have overcome them, because the one who is in You, is greater than the one who is in the world.

Lesson 2: Identify your strengths and use them
1st John 4:19: We love because God first loved us, don't focus on yourself; instead focus on the awesome love that God has for you.

Lesson 3: United efforts reap better rewards
1st Thessalonians 3: 12-13: May the Lord make your love increase and overflow for each other, and everyone else. May He strengthen your hearts. so that you will be blameless and holy in the presence of our God and Father when our Lord Jesus comes with all His holy ones. A great team effort and maturity to pool resources insured victory for the hare and the tortoise.

Matthew 18: 20: "For where two or three gather together as my followers, I am there among them.

It is my sincere prayer, as we've gathered as a mature body of believers through prayer and supplication we can win this race.

It is in Jesus name I pray, Amen.

FIRST FRUIT GOD REMEMBER

Jesus, Thank You, for the cross and the resurrection. It was a turning point for us as creation.

O' God, your death was for our sins, buried and rose again on the third day. all you promised as in 1st Corinthians 15:3. Jesus, You willingly suffered and died by crucifixion as the ultimate sacrifice for our sins 1st John 1:10.

Jesus, You had victory over sin and death in your resurrection for all who believe; Romans 6:5. O', God today would you appear to us as Bad Friday. But "*oh no*" this was the ultimate life insurance plan for us, to save your people from their sins. Thank You!

Saints, in order for the good news of the gospel to be understood by us, we have to understand the bad news as a sinful people. Thank You, Jesus, for an opportunity for deliverance, with the chance at Jesus' grace. Hallelujah and relief through salvation, glory to God!

God, Your wrath against sin had to be made manifest for forgiveness and salvation. Hallelujah for your people. So, without that awful day of suffering, sorrow and shed blood at the cross, God could not be both "just and the justifier" of those who trust Jesus.

So, saints, this day seems evil is actually the knockout blow in God's grand plan to redeem the world from bondage. So, thank God for the resurrection.

It is in Jesus name I pray, Amen.

FIRST FRUIT GOD REMEMBER

Paraphrased: O,' Lord, thank You for your righteousness; we will praise your name.

Psalm 7:17. Thank You, Lord for great mercy, birth into a living hope through the resurrection of Jesus Christ.

Thank You, Lord, for the realization salvation is not death, it's right now for those who believe.

Thank You, Lord, for the excitement of faith, not letting it fade away. David said this, "Restore to me the joy of my salvation" Psalm 51:12.

Thank You, Lord, for not losing heart even though our flesh is wasting away.

Thank You, for a renewing of our inside's day by day.

So, Lord, keep our eyes in the spirit seeing eternally, 2nd Corinthians 4:16-18.

So, beloved, praise God because of His mercy in our great salvation.

It is in Jesus name I pray, Amen.

FIRST FRUIT GOD REMEMBER

THANK YOU, FOR THE RAIN GOD, THE HARVEST IN JAMES 5:7, AND ACTS 2:16-17.

Saints, the Bible refers to the latter rain as a symbolic meaning of the end time Harvest of souls into God's kingdom. Thank You, for the blessings in the rain, in the poplar trees, Isaiah 44:3-4.

Elijah heard the sound of rushing rain by faith because God spoke to him. So, before he even prayed, Elijah declared God's word as a fact. God bless us with water poured down from the sky. Because your word stands forever, so let the rain fall.

God Thank You, for the life force in the rain making plants grow. When times are hard, drench us God for better versions of us; that's just part of the deal. So, saints, let's try to make it rain, seeding the clouds. Rain gives us life. We need it. Denzel Washington once said *"**You pray for rain you gotta deal with the mud too.**"*

It is in Jesus name I pray, Amen

FIRST FRUIT GOD REMEMBER

Beloved, the penal substitution theory teaches that Jesus suffered the penalty for mankind's sins. It's the idea that divine forgiveness must satisfy divine justice. meaning that God is not willing or able to just forgive sin without requiring a satisfaction for it. Oh, but the Word occurs in the Romans 5:11, which means to reconcile, in the Old Testament, Hebrews atonement. Thank You, Jesus, for John 17:1-26.

Thank You, Jesus, for Romans 8:1-39; "There is, therefore, now no condemnation for those who are in Christ Jesus.

Thank You, Jesus, for Romans 5:18, "Therefore, as one trespass led to condemnation for all men, so one act of righteousness leads to justification and life for all men.

Thank You, God, for Isaiah 53,4-6, Isaiah 53:11-12.

So, God, as You wrote in Revelation 1:8. "I am the Alpha and the Omega" says the Lord God, 'who is and who was and who is to come, the Almighty". The devil wants to break us down, he wants us to be convinced, there's something left for us to do to be like God, that we have to keep trying to be loving, kind, patient, all (that He is but we already are)

It is in Jesus name I pray, Amen.

FIRST FRUIT GOD REMEMBER

Thank You, God, for when we feel small, extraordinary things are possible.

Jeremiah 29:11 "For I know the plans I have for you, declares the Lord, plans to prosper you and not harm you, plans to give you hope and a future.

Lord, we thank You for Esther 4:14.

Perhaps you were born for such a time as this. Jesus, You said, "And we know that for those who love God, all things work together for good, for those who are called according to his purpose. Romans 8:28.

Thank You, God for, it's not what it looks like. Psalm 33:11, Jeremiah 1:5, 2nd Peter 3:9, Psalm 32:8. It's not our reasonableness, do not be anxious about anything, set your minds on things that are above, not on things that are on the earth.

It is in Jesus name I pray, Amen.

FIRST FRUIT GOD REMEMBER

O, Lord, thank You for conviction! A constant reminder for those that believe the Lord is continually refining us and touching our hearts. Lord, we pray that the Holy Spirit always shows us areas in our lives that are displeasing. Lord, help us be open to the Holy Spirit for guidance.

John 16:8 "When He comes, He will prove the world to be in the wrong about sin and righteousness, and of the coming judgement."

Lord, help us not to ignore conviction and do nothing about it. I repent and do better. Thank You for the reconciliation that comes with repentance. The Holy Spirit exposes the evil within, so conviction is good; it saves our souls on a daily basis and makes an image of Christ.

I'm paraphrasing, 2 Kings 22:19: "Lord, give us that humbled heart"!

It is in Jesus name I pray, Amen.

FIRST FRUIT GOD REMEMBER

Mankind
He has told you what's good and what it is the Lord requires of you, "to act justly, to love mercy, to walk humbly with your God, Micah 6:8.

Thank You, for the blessing of being merciful so that we may receive mercy. O', God, the world is saturated in sin, but You said because judgement without mercy will be shown to anyone who has not been merciful. Mercy triumphs over judgement, James 2:13.

Please help us be merciful, just as your Father is merciful.
Help us be patient.
Help anyone around you who is hurting.
Give people a second chance:
    do good to those who hurt you,
    be kind to those who offend you,
    build love bridges for the unpopular
    value relationships over rules.

The first step in the process of mercy is to be just. Show us, Father, what a spiritual work of mercy is. Works of mercy sometime known as acts of mercy (practice it). Corporate works of mercy, concerning the material and physical needs of others. Spiritual works of mercy, this concerns the spiritual needs of others.

The Lord Almighty says, "administer real justice; show real mercy and compassion to one another, don't oppress the word mercy. It appears in the Bible 174 times. So, in Jesus' name from Genesis to Revelation, let's learn how to be merciful.

It is in Jesus name I pray, Amen.

FIRST FRUIT GOD REMEMBER

1st Peter 2:9: "But you are a chosen race, a royal priesthood, a holy nation, a people for His own possession, that you may proclaim the excellencies of Him who called you out of darkness into the marvelous light.

Thank You, Lord, for Ephesians 5:8: "For at one time you were darkness, but now you are light in the Lord, walk as children of light.

Thank You, Lord, for freedom in Christ that has set us free; standing firm and not submitting to a yoke of slavery; Galatians 5:1.

The Bible states we are created in the image of God. Saints, the revelation of race might start in Genesis, it does not start with a special race of people.

Adam and Eve are not Hebrew or Egyptians, they are not White, Black, or Semitic, which is an old word not used anymore. (Their) Adam and Eve's ethnicity isn't even mentioned (because they were born as adults and created, not born) The Bible to stress that they are mother and father of all peoples of all ethnicities.

Thank You, God, for Genesis 1:26 where you said, "Let us make man [Adam] in our image according to our likeness and 1:27 describes what you did. Thank You for the images of you male, and female, sharing mental and spiritual faculties.

People share with God an appointment of humankind as God's representatives on Earth, a capacity to relate to God. Consider this a spectacular blessing saints.

So, with this being written Beloved, both dignity and equality of human beings are traced in Scripture to our creation to think one race or ethnicity is superior to another race is a denial of the fact that all people are created in the image of God.

It is in Jesus name I pray, Amen.

FIRST FRUIT GOD REMEMBER

Thank you, God, for the revelation of you in nature. Nature testifies to God's existence.

Apostle Paul wrote to the church in Rome; Romans 1:19-20 about the awesomeness of the universe! Beloved, he gives testimony to God.

Thank you, God, for Psalm 19:1-6. Beloved, God's glory is proclaimed. Look up when you go outside today. Thank you! the heavens are declaring God's glory, a sign to humanity that He exists.

Beloved, the testimony is always about God's power and majesty. Each and every day; night after night! Don't let the devil fool you. Humanity is always reminded of God's existence. The revelation isn't in words in nature. but the heavens give a silent testimony.

Beloved, all people everywhere can see the revelation in nature's form; no geographical walls, no language walls, every language for all nations who believe. God is revealing himself. The sun representing the son; shining to God's existence and His love. Nothing hides from the sun. No one can hide from God. Romans :18-21, speaks of God's revelation through nature.

God, thank you for the silent witness of yourself for everyone.
Beloved, we pray for the scales to be removed!

It is in Jesus name I pray, Amen

First Fruit God Remember

NO GUTS NO GLORY JOB 16:12

God has made me his target; his archers surround me. Genesis 6:6 angry God.

Isaiah 38:16-17. In the world "no guts, no glory", an American Air Force General Frederick Corbin Blesse wrote a manual about air-to-air combat, Published, 1955, Guts, Judges 11:1 Warrior.

Thank you, God, for using the weak a lot, the unexpected, and the so called undeserving, the undesirable, whoremongers, recovering addicts, the humble, the poor, the last to be picked, or someone just like us. Matthew 5:3-12.

Blessed are the poor in spirit, for theirs is the kingdom of heaven. Beloved, the Hebrew word used for glory means heaviness or weight. In the Old Testament in Greek, the word doxa, means glory. Glory has different meanings, but I like splendor, power, the brightness of God.

Do all things for the glory of God 1st Corinthians 10:31.
God, we thank you for Romans 14:23: "Do everything for the glory of God". Thank you, God, for the life in your words.

God, we're so thankful because your words teach us your will. Thank you for our hearts, Jesus, to know, and believe, you are a spirit. This is the small voice we hear. Thank you, Jesus, for guidance on what you're doing and what you've done, and what you're going to do.

It is in Jesus name I pray, Amen.

FIRST FRUIT GOD REMEMBER

O',God, you made adult bones hard and brittle and more likely to break than bend. 1st Corinthians 13:11 states saints: "When I was a child, I talked like a child, I thought like a child, I reasoned like a child. When I became a man, I put the ways of childhood behind me.

O,' God, help us remember children's bones are different from adult bones. Help us understand when it comes to treating fractures in children, they are not small adults. So, with knowing this saints, it affects the type of care they need to heal properly.

Father, thank You. As adults we have 206 bones, but God, You made babies with three hundred bones in their bodies. Thank You for this advantage in a child, Lord!

Saints, this means if a broken bone is crooked, it can straighten itself out over time, in a child. God, thank You for Matthew 19:14: Jesus said, "Let the children alone, and do not hinder them from coming to me; for the kingdom of heaven belongs to such as these.

God, help us chase after the things that are peaceful and the things that edify one another as in Romans 14:19.

Edify with our love 1st Corinthians 8:1
Edify with our gifts Ephesians 4:11-12.
Edify with our hope 1st Thessalonians 5:11.
Edify with our testimony acts 9:31.
Edify with our words Ephesians 4: 15-16

FIRST FRUIT GOD REMEMBER

"He will command His angels concerning you to guard you in all your ways", Psalm 91:11 .

In modern folklore, Santa Claus is said to make a list of children throughout the world. He categorizes them according to their behavior. He then sets out to deliver presents, including toys and candy, to all the well-behaved children in the world. misbehaving children receive coal on the night of Christmas eve.

Folk is the traditions, beliefs, customs, and stories of a community, passed through generations by word of mouth. Then there are angels-celestial go-betweens, God or heaven and humanity, protectors and guides for humans, and servants of God.

Passages in Ezekiel 1: 1-28 and Ezekiel 10:20 give descriptions of angels. Angels are mentioned 273 times in the Bible.

Isaiah 6:1-7: seraphim are the highest angelic class, they are the caretakers of God's throne, and are always shouting Holy, Holy, Holy, the Lord of Host; the whole earth is full of His glory!

Duties assigned to angels include communicating revelations from God, glorifying God, recording every person's action , and taking a person's soul at the time of death. "He will command his angels concerning you. to guard you in all your ways", Psalm 91:11.

O, God, thank you for truth and Jesus as our Savior, no magic, no folklore needed to have a relationship with Christ; from the heart seek righteousness and confess with your mouth salvation; Romans 10:13: "Whoever calls upon the name of the Lord will be saved.

O, God no toys, no candy, no coal; Joshua 24:14-15
Merry Christmas!
It is in Jesus name I pray, Amen.

FIRST FRUIT GOD REMEMBER

Fear is a liar: "Let us not become weary in doing good, for at the proper time we will reap a harvest if we do not give up". Galatians 6:9 NIV

Father, help us turn to you when we feel like giving up.
Father, remind us that good things take work and help us remember it takes a lot of work!
Father, help us know even the efforts aren't fruitless.
Saints, there is a hymn titled, "The Hymn of Promise, #707, by Natalie Sleeth.
It's about an apple seed, how a whole tree is inside a little bitty seed. But saints, you can't just crack the seed open and have a whole tree pop out. It takes time, patience, nurturing, and protection. Saints, when you reap that harvest from those seeds, it is so worth the effort!

Hebrews 12:1 "Therefore, since we are surrounded by such a great cloud of witnesses, let's throw off everything that hinders and the sin that so easily entangles, and let us run with perseverance the race marked out for us in God's word.

So, Father, we declare as it is written in Your word, you can do hard things, "I can do all this through him who gives me strength." Philippians 4:4

It is in Jesus name I pray, Amen.

FIRST FRUIT GOD REMEMBER

Isaiah 46:4: I am He who will sustain you.

O' God, strengthen our relationship with the Holy Spirit; help us know who we are.

O' God, help us dwell in the Father's love every morning.
O' God help, us to have those conversations with the Holy Spirit.
O' God help us, to notice the Holy Spirit's whispers and nudges.
O' God, bring to our minds how the Holy Spirit nudged and spoke in the past.
O' God, help us think of the Holy Spirit as we just be quiet and listen. O' God, thank You for the reality there is no formula, but the more time we spend with You, the stronger our relationship gets.

Now God, we thank You for the hovering, whispering, nudging, even when we're barely awake or aware of His presence.

Time to wake up-in the name of Jesus name I pray, Amen.

FIRST FRUIT GOD REMEMBER

Father God, thank you for the donkeys.
King David, King Solomon, Jesus, and all the prophets never rode horses, they always rode donkeys.

Thank You for the Cross that appears on a donkey's back, even the dark donkeys! Thy cross I'll carry the legend of the Jerusalem donkey. It's said that the Nubian donkey has a cross; because this breed of donkey carried Jesus to Jerusalem on Palm Sunday, seeing the tragedy of Jesus' crucifixion, the donkey wished he could carry the cross for and bear his burden.

Thank you Lord for Numbers 22:28: "Then the Lord opened the donkey's mouth and said to Balaam, "What have I done to you to make you beat me these three times?" God, help us be consistent with our actions, not easily fooled. Do we obey God willingly or do we grudgingly, or with impure motives? Help us, God, to love from obedience and nothing else.

It is in Jesus name I pray, Amen.

FIRST FRUIT GOD REMEMBER

Jesus thank you for 1st John 1:7. Every word in the english language ending with "eth means to continue. Jesus thank you for the blood as it contains its cleaning power in our lives daily. When we accept you in our hearts. Thank you lord for the blood spilled on calvary that didn't run into the ground; thank you lord for taking it all with you. Thank you for the glory walk and the offering on the altar of god. Thank you for no limits of the blood. Thank you for plenty of blood for everybody. The limit comes when we as people don't use the blood. Thank you for the blood, like god's love is eternal. Like god's faith, there is no lack in the blood. It is impossible for heaven to run out of the love,faith, joy, peace, compassion, and patience, we need in the blood. Thank god for the blood that stained the old cross and seals our hearts. It is in Jesus name I pray, Amen.

FIRST FRUIT GOD REMEMBER

Matthew 25:35, I was hungry and you gave me something to eat. I was thirsty, and you gave me something to drink. I was a stranger, and you took me into your home. Oh father, thank you for a charitable heart as you have done it unto the world. God thank you for a light opportunity to be devoted to my brothers and sisters in love. Thank you god for it is more blessed to give than to receive spirit. Oh god it is word to sacrifice for others, and I want to do what you would have me to do. Oh god we want the money bags that do not get old, with the promises that don't fail, we want those heavenly treasures were no thief will approach us and moth does not destroy! As Luke 12:33. Father god, thank you for selflessness and not pride,give us a desire god to be humble and honorable. Thank you father for not just being interested in our lives, but the lives of others. It is in Jesus name I pray, Amen.

FIRST FRUIT GOD REMEMBER

O'God, thank You for Your firm word and promises for us as Your people.

Psalm 93:5 states: "Your statutes, Lord, stand firm; holiness ado to endless days. Thank You, God for Philippians 4:1-2; "Therefore, my dear brothers, and sisters whom I long for, my joy and my victors crown. Thank You, God, for courageous and strong faith. Thank You, God, for the win, Luke 21:19, standing firm in life according to Your word.

Thank You, God, for not being made secure in sickness, but the root of righteousness is immovable. O' God, You said in James 1:2-4: "Consider it nothing but joy when You fall into all sorts of trails, know the testing of faith produces endurance".

It is in Jesus name I pray, Amen.

FIRST FRUIT, GOD REMEMBER

O' God, throughout life, the enemy has whispered labels in our ears, when we say we identified with and call ourselves this, not that. Thank You, God, that You have called us new creations. In Your Word, You said, "Therefore, if anyone is in Christ, he is a new creation, the old has passed away; behold, the new has come." 2nd Corinthians 5:7

We say or have said, we are scarred; but God says, "we are healed." Isaiah 53:5 Thank You, God, for deliverance from when we are weak, saying that, but this is what God says, "He makes us strong." Psalm 18:32.

Thank You, God, for deliverance from when we say we are abandoned. God says, "we are adopted." Ephesians 1:5.

Thank You, God, for deliverance when we say we've been rejected. God says, "we are his!" Isaiah 43:1

Thank You, God, for deliverance when we say we are alone; God says, He is always with us. Joshua 1:9.

Thank You, God, for deliverance when we say we are hopeless; God says because of Him, we are hopeful. Jeremiah 29:11

Thank You, God, for deliverance when we say we are purposeless; God says we were created with a purpose. Esther 4:14.

Thank You, God, for deliverance when we say we have failed; God says we are victorious in Christ. 1st Corinthians 15:57.

Thank You, God, for deliverance when we say we are lost, God says, "He gives us direction". Isaiah 30:21.

Thank You, God, for deliverance when we say we are worried, anxious, and afraid; God says, with Him, we are peace-filled. John 14:27.

Thank You, God, for deliverance when we say, we are unhappy; God says, we are joyful and joy-filled. John 15:11.

Thank You, God, for deliverance when we say we are afraid; God says we are powerful, loved, and have a sound mind. 2nd Timothy 1:7.

Thank You, God, for deliverance when we say we are nothing special; God says, we are fearfully and wonderfully made. Psalm 139:14.

Thank You, God, for deliverance when we say we are worthless; God says, "Jesus died because we are worth it." John 3:16

I declare right now Saints of God, from today forward you will not speak the negative and believe this: God said, You are the **this and** not the **negative that you've spoken into Your life**.

It is in Jesus name I pray, Amen.

FIRST FRUIT GOD REMEMBER

So, Jesus said to him, "Unless you see signs and wonders, you will not believe. Heavenly Father, thank You for your works and your wonders You made known; Your power among the people. Thank, You, God, for the natural order, compassion to meet our human needs as in Mark 1:41.

Thank You for your affirmation as being the Son of God. Through your miracles, wonders, and signs: Acts 2:22. God, please grant us an obedient faith to see the world supernaturally to come.

Acts of God to illuminate our dark places in the middle of miracles just when we think this life is all there is. O' God, we desire an introduction to the spiritual reality of the presence of you!

It is in Jesus name I pray, Amen.

FIRST FRUIT GOD REMEMBER

Psalm 118:17: "I shall not die, but live, and declare the works of the Lord".

Hebrews 12:29: for our God is a consuming fire.

O', God, thank You for John's water baptism, but it is You, Lord, that baptizes us with the Holy Spirit and with fire.

O; God it is you with messengers of winds and ministers a flaming fire. Jeremiah 23:29, You said. "Is not my Word like fire, declares the Lord, and like a hammer that breaks the rock in pieces?"

Thank You, Lord, for our passing through the water, You are there, and through rivers, You're there. Thank You, Lord, for not letting us be overwhelmed. Thank You, Lord, for bringing us through fires without burns, and flames that consume us!

It is in Jesus name I pray, Amen.

FIRST FRUIT GOD REMEMBER

1st Peter 5:10: "And after you have suffered a little while, the God of all grace, who has called you to his eternal glory in Christ, will Himself restore, confirm, strengthen, and establish you. A recipe for a spiritual punch for thanksgiving, not a drink, but a movement of thanks in Jesus' name.

"Thanks" is used in the Old Testament 102 times conceptually and is used 72 times "acknowledging what is right about God in praise and thanksgiving

1st Chronicles 16:34: "Thank, You, God, for being the center of my thankfulness. Thank You, O, God, for opening the gates of righteousness as in Psalm 118:19, "I will glory in the Lord; let the afflicted hear and rejoice, glorify the Lord with me; let us exalt His name together; Psalm 34:1-3, Psalm 106:1.

Enduring love: Hebrews 12:28-29, (God)
A consuming fire: Hebrews 13:15
Fruits from your lips: Psalm 107:21
Deeds for mankind,
Psalm 69:30 glorifying God's name
Colossians 3:16: sing psalms and spiritual hymns.

It is in Jesus name I pray, Amen.

FIRST FRUIT GOD REMEMBER

O', God, thank You for being spirit, not physical blood, but spiritual blood-the Holy Spirit; not touching physical blood, because physical blood cannot touch the soul.

God, thank You for your spiritual blood, not limited by time and space. O', God, the life of a man is in his blood; when the blood stops flowing, he dies. Your life God is the Holy Spirit-there can be no spiritual life.

O' God, teach us this in John 3:6; this means the spiritual man cannot be quickened by the natural Holy Spirit; Hebrews 9:14.

Thank You, God, for John 7:37-38; that living water is the Holy Spirit shed blood.
Thank You, for Matthew 26:28 and the symbolism, but thank you, Jesus, for the day of Pentecost Acts 2:33.

Please, God, continue to impart your blood.

It is in Jesus name I pray, Amen.

FIRST FRUIT GOD REMEMBER

God, thank You, for choice, free will.

1st Corinthians 10:13 and 2nd Peter 3-9, "the Lord is not slow in keeping His promise, as some understand slowness. instead, He is patient with you, not wanting anyone to perish, but everyone to reach repentance

Thank you, God, for teaching us about free will in Matthew 23:37 and Revelation 22:17.

God, you've given us Deuteronomy 30:19 - calling heaven and earth to witness the choice we make, choose life. In Christ there is judgement, also 2nd Corinthians 5:10. We will receive what we deserve, according to everything we've done, good or bad in our bodily life. So, help us God to make right choices today, accepting Jesus as our Lord and Savior, then we will be transformed to run from sin and love righteousness. This saints, is called the "miracle of conversion".

I pray we accept the advantage of God's gift of free will and choose life, and the strength that comes with the Holy Spirit to work in the light, to be a part of the rain; nonstop at the appointed time in God's heavenly glory.

It is in Jesus name I pray, Amen.

FIRST FRUIT GOD REMEMBER

Thank You heavenly Father for the courage of being human.
Thank you, Father for the struggles in the fruit.
Thank you, Father for motherhood; Philippians 1:3. I thank my God in all remembrance of your mother. Proverbs 31:25 "She is clothed with strength and dignity; she can laugh at the days to come".

John 10:27: "My sheep hear my voice, and I know them, and they follow me".

Psalms 119:18: "Open thou mine eyes, that I may behold wondrous things out of Thy law".

Psalm 119:105: Thy word is a lamp unto my feet, and a light unto my path.

Exodus 20:12: Honor thy father and thy mother; that thy days may be long upon the land which the Lord thy God giveth thee.

Proverbs 20:11: "Even a child is known by his doings, whether his work be pure, and whether it be right".

Philippians 4:4 "Rejoice in the Lord always and again I say, rejoice.

It is in Jesus name I pray, Amen.

FIRST FRUIT GOD REMEMBER

Proverbs 17:22: A cheerful heart is good medicine, but a crushed spirit dries up the bones.

Ezekiel 37: Thank You Lord for bringing us out by your spirit and setting us in the valley.

Thank you, Lord for leading us back and forth in those dry bone places.
Thank you, Lord for asking us can a dry bone live?
Thank you, for the prophecy to those bones from as human beings.
Thank you, Lord, for teaching us to say "dry bones hear the word of the Lord"
I will make breath, I enter you and you will come to life.
I will attach tendons to you and make flesh come on you and cover you with skin
I will breathe in you, and then you will know that I am the Lord.

Thank you Lord for the revelation of bones and their indestructible symbolism. Thank you for Ezekiel, the African prophet of hope.

It is in Jesus name I pray, Amen.

FIRST FRUIT GOD REMEMBER

Thank you, God, for being a property owner with a promise instead of a mortgage! for those who believe. In the world to own a mansion, you'll need an income of about $100,000 annually to afford a mansion of 5,0000 square feet, which is considered small in every state. But in heaven, there is no income requirement for only a relationship with God. God's mansion, shining with the glory of God, and a brilliance like a precious jewel like jasper, clear as crystal. high walls, twelve gates and twelve angels at the gates, a place of peace, love, community, and worship.

Thank you for not one mansion, but many!
John 14:2-3, heaven is a city built for worship
Hebrews 12:22-23, heaven is filled with peace, joy, and praise.

Beloved, I choose God's community. And it is in Jesus name I pray, you'll choose the same, Amen.

FIRST FRUIT GOD REMEMBER

Thank You, God, for using disabilities to show your awesome love for all creation. Thank You, God, for helping us as humanity to understand we should imitate that love. God, help us not to take things for granted.

God, You remain perfect, good, loving, kind, and fair. There are people who are blind, who see better than people with eyesight. There are deaf people, who can hear better than people that have good hearing.

Sometimes the things we can't change end up changing us. There is no greater disability in society, than the inability to see a person as more. "Robert M. Hensel, "the only disability in life is a bad attitude." Your disability will never make God love you less. "Put go in front of disabled, it spells , "God is able." Nick Vujicic

Thank you, God, for:
John 9:2-4
Exodus 4:10-12
Psalm 139:13-14
Isaiah 55:9
Leviticus 19:14
Luke 14:12-14

Beloved, hope will not disappoint us, because God's love has been poured out in the hearts of those that believe through the Holy Spirit who was given to us.

It is in Jesus name I pray, Amen.

FIRST FRUIT GOD REMEMBER

"Shaken, not stirred "they know nothing, they understand nothing; they walk about in darkness, all the foundations of the earth are shaken," Psalm 82:5.

The world is a mess right now, and when we see or hear about it, we're usually shaken, but as believers; life offers us some stuff that's a lot different from the world. Therefore, since we are receiving a kingdom that cannot be shaken, let's be thankful, and worship God willingly with reverence, and excitement," for our God is a consuming fire" , Hebrews 12:28-29 .

When Jesus entered Jerusalem the entire city was stirred and asked, "who is this?" the crowd answered," this is Jesus, the prophet from Nazareth in Galilee, Matthew 21:10-11.

Beloved, when the Lord is present, hearts are stirred, we need to be stirred in the presence of the Holy Spirit. as it moves through the church, which is us. That's when great things begin to happen.

Haggai 1:14, the miraculous takes place beloved; God's kingdom is built up, souls are saved deliverance over destruction, seek the Lord for his move to take place in us.

It is in Jesus name I pray, Amen.

FIRST FRUIT GOD REMEMBER

Beloved, "to remember" used in Hebrew, means "God's movement toward fulfillment of a particular promise." When God remembers you, your tears will be turned to joy. When God remembers you, the unimaginable, unexpected, uncommon miracles will happen. When God remembers, your obstacles will be rolled away, and barriers will be broken.

Beloved, "God wins'", is a response provoking questions; love wins-raises; and we thank You God, for your response. Philippians 4:13. "I can do all things through Him who strengthens me.

1st Corinthians 15:57: "But thanks be to God, who gives us the victory through Our Lord Jesus Christ

Luke 18:2: "What is impossible with men, is possible with God".
Matthew 20:16
Deuteronomy 20:4
Galatians 6:9
Romans 10:13

It is in Jesus name, I pray, Amen.

FIRST FRUIT GOD REMEMBER

God, thank You for deliverance from the spirit of pride. Help us God not to be wise in our own eyes. Thank you, God, for seeking humility and a will to learn from You and others.

Beloved, people who struggle with pride also struggle with greed. Blessings are poured out on those who are generous. Galatians 6:4 reads "Each one should test their actions, then they can take pride in themselves alone, without comparing themselves to someone else.

James 4:6, reads beloved, "but he gives us more grace"; that is why Scripture reads: "God opposes the proud, but shows favor to the humble. Pride always exalts himself above God. Pride kills your love for God, kills your passion for God. Pride is behind every sin ever committed, every rebellion against God and His Word, and every fall of the heart of a person, from the loving embrace of his Creator.

God, deliver the world from haughtiness; James 4:6, 1st Peter 5:5, and deliver us. Isaiah 66:2.

It is in Jesus name I pray, Amen.

FIRST FRUIT GOD REMEMBER

Thank, You, Jesus for the *__fruit__* of the Spirit, not *__fruits.__*

Thank, You, for simultaneously magnifying Grace! When I walk in the Spirit, the Spirit gives me the character of Jesus and He is consistent.

Thank, You, for real grace, because the fruit of the Spirit will give me full access to Jesus by faith.

The Spirit imparts the full life of Jesus!

Thank, You, for real fruit.

Beloved, a life in Christ is not imitation. Christ's fruit comes from the impartation of the Spirit.

So Beloved, it's all or nothing.

It is in Jesus name I pray, Amen.

FIRST FRUIT GOD REMEMBER

Beloved, we all probably know the general meaning of the word fulfilled: to finish or reach the end of something. Oh but, thank God for the importance of the word fulfilled to the believer. we've been taught in your Word God, without this word for us in Christ we would lose it! Thank You God for salvation, full or filled up; John 3:16.

Thank You, God, for your only begotten son; no animal sacrifice for our sins. Hebrews 10:4: Lord, you know we are not perfect and when we make promises, we may fall short.

O, God, help us to be careful in our unfulfilled promises. Help our **"yes" to be yes and our "no" to be no**. Matthew 5:36-37

Thank you, God, for your always yes; not telling us to do something contradictory to your nature; "He cannot deny himself", 2nd Timothy 2:13. God, help us fulfill our promises. It is in Jesus name I pray, Amen.

FIRST FRUIT GOD REMEMBER

O', God thank you for the revelation of looking saved and living saved, two different things. So, don't judge people.

Thank, You, God, for the hard lesson that it's more important to have an inward knowing than to have an outward showing. So, God, thank, You, for a free sons now existence as it is written in Romans 8:14-16. no longer slaves to fear or death! God, thank You, for being an heir and your children. to go through my trials and face my past. O', God receiving my inheritance of God; Romans 8:17.

Thank you God for the journey. I will not be destroyed by my failures or controlled by my past mistakes. Because of Calvary, I have been reconciled by the redeeming blood of Jesus Christ. I must share my testimonies of my past to the glory of God, knowing that all things do work together for good.

It is in Jesus name I pray, Amen.

FIRST FRUIT GOD REMEMBER

"The spirit of God hath made me, and the breath of the Almighty hath given me life". Jacob 33:4.

O', God, thank You for being made, this word means force, cause to move forward in this context. Thank you, God, for changing the way we speak to our challenges. Thank You for not cursing the trail. O', God, but saying this is for my strength.

O', God, thank You for the blessing in disguise.
Thank You God, for not running from opposition.
Thank you, O' God, for divine reversal.

It is in Jesus name I pray, Amen.

FIRST FRUIT GOD REMEMBER

PSALM 117

Praise the Lord all you nations, extol him, all you people, for great is his love toward us, and the faithfulness of the Lord endures forever, praise the Lord!

O', God, guide me in my decisions, early will I seek you", Psalm 63:1.

O', God, thank You for the gift of today knowing I am alive on this earth for a reason. Thank You, God, for my Nehemiah experiences during this season in my life.

O', God, please continue to help me seek you early before I come up with my own plan.

O', God, help us to teach each new generation to seek you first, so that our children will know your truth God and your power at an early age.; "Train up a child in the way he should go, and when he is old he will not depart from it" Proverbs 22:6. Seek the Lord early.

It is in the name of Jesus, I pray, Amen.

FIRST FRUIT GOD REMEMBER

Ephesians 2:10: "For we are his workmanship created in Christ Jesus for good works ,which God prepared beforehand, that we should walk in them".

O', God, thank You for the Psalms because this book is for the soul! Father, your psalms cover all aspects of a person as a whole.

O', God, You wrote in Psalm 63 about the whole person, six characteristics of prayer and worship in David.

Thank You, God , for David's connection in his heart, spirit, will, thoughts, feelings, body, his friendships, and soul.

Father God bless me with a true understanding of these precepts, transforming me to be the whole person to be more like Christ.

It is in Jesus name I pray, Amen.

FIRST FRUIT GOD REMEMBER

O', God, help me stand in the gap, to help others flow in things above and level out my peaks and valleys, placing my faith actively in you, loving others without judgement, obeying in His timing, worshiping with a thankful heart.

Thank You O', God, for recognizing my season right now mountain top or desert. O', God, I repent for being in a desert, knowing you can use that desert place to grow me, and mold me to be more like you. And God, help all of us to realize this desert experience will pass in your time.

O', God, thank You because I know that in all things you work for the good of us that love you, and have been called according to your purpose, as you wrote in Romans 8:28.

So, God, it is my sincere desire to do what You commanded, and not turn right or left but look to the hills because our help comes from You as I seek the mountain top experience .

It is in Jesus name I pray, Amen.

FIRST FRUIT GOD REMEMBER

O' Lord, thank You for the other believers in my life. I ask that we get closer to You together.
Will you help our relationships grow in honesty and love?
Heavenly Father, I ask that we build each other up in Your name, and help us, O' God to be your hands and feet to each other and to the world, and in the earth.

O' God, bring us to remembrance of our Goshen place. As you wrote in Genesis 45:10. "You shall dwell in the land of Goshen, and you shall be near me, you and your children and your children's children and your flocks, your herds, and all that you have. O', God, I declare in the mighty name of Jesus that everyone be taken right now to a Goshen place.; place of comfort and plenty.

It is in Jesus name I pray, Amen.

FIRST FRUIT GOD REMEMBER

1st Corinthians 6:19, do you not know that your body is a temple of the Holy Spirit within you, whom you have from God? you are not your own.

O', God, thank You for the wind, fire, water, and the oil; scriptural symbols for your spirit God.

Thank You, O' God, for the gift of the spirit, I'm blessed to have as a Christian soul.

Thank You, God for breath, that is spirit, wind as air in motion.

Thank You, O', God, for spirit, and life-two words for one thing.

O', God, I thank You for a rushing mighty wind to set loose the highest work of spiritual supernatural life.

Thank you, O; God for no lies that man tries to put on me. You are God all by yourself, without limitations, and I praise and rejoice in that Lord. Hallelujah! To God be the glory!

It is in Jesus name I pray, Amen.

First Fruit God Remember

Chasing the Fruit Tree

Thank you, Jesus!
John 15: The vine draws nourishment from the root and sends that nourishment into the branches so they can bear fruit.

This means that the spiritual life is not our work; and the fruit we bear is not ours either. It's God's work in us.

WRITTEN BY: VICKIE KNOX

Special Thanks:
Matthew 19:26

But Jesus beheld their thoughts, and said unto them, With men this is impossible; but if they forsake all things for my sake, with God whatsoever things I speak are possible.

1. Mr. Nick Caya, and Team W-2K
2. Doctor Vivan St. Cloud
3. Shamille, and Royale McCullough
4. Mr. Terry Mitchell
5. Ms. Julia Church
6. Mr. and Mrs. Butch, and Jackie Tanner
7. Rev. Render Russell, and Family
8. Ms. Mary Battle
9. Pastor Micheal E. Sutton Sr./ Dixie Hills First Baptist Church
10. Mrs. Robin Carey and Family
11. Ms. Jasmine Carter and Jamir Davis
12. Doctor Detrius Jones and Family
13. LaTasha Arnold, and Mr, Tyson Jackson
14. Mrs. Carolyn Chambliss
15. The Jones Family
16. Marian, and Annett Wise
17. Mrs. Cookie Gunn
18. Just Pray Ministries/Pastor's Oscar and Regina Williams
19. Ms. Emily Wise
20. Ms. Pat Render
21. Mrs. Ronda and Family
22. Prophetess Meliza Woodward
23. Team FedEx South Cobb Pkwy

www.ingramcontent.com/pod-product-compliance
Lightning Source LLC
Chambersburg PA
CBHW070849160426
43192CB00012B/2367